Dakota Fanning

ABDO
Publishing Company

Big Buddy BOOKS
Buddy Bios

by **Sarah Tieck**

VISIT US AT
www.abdopublishing.com

Published by ABDO Publishing Company, 8000 West 78th Street, Edina, Minnesota 55439.

Printed in the United States of America, North Mankato, Minnesota.
112009
012010
 PRINTED ON RECYCLED PAPER

Coordinating Series Editor: Rochelle Baltzer
Contributing Editors: Heidi M.D. Elston, Megan M. Gunderson, BreAnn Rumsch, Marcia Zappa
Graphic Design: Maria Hosley
Cover Photograph: *AP Photo*: Chris Pizzello
Interior Photographs/Illustrations: *AP Photo*: Tammie Arroyo (p. 25), Kevork Djansezian (p. 18), Jennifer Graylock
     (p. 25), Chris Haston/NBCU Photo Bank AP Images (p. 8), Nam Y. Huh (p. 17), Rick Malman (p. 21), Luis
     Martinez (p. 23), Chris Pizzello (pp. 5, 27), Reed Saxon (p. 13), Matt Sayles (p. 28), Paul Skipper (p. 15), Kathy
     Willens (p. 17); *Getty Images*: Jeff Kravitz/FilmMagic (p. 26), Chris Pizzello/WireImage (p. 11), Alberto E.
     Rodriguez (p. 15), Sgranitz/WireImage (p. 7); *iStockphoto.com*: ©iStockphoto.com/ekash (p. 11).

Library of Congress Cataloging-in-Publication Data

Tieck, Sarah, 1976-
  Dakota Fanning : talented actress / Sarah Tieck.
    p. cm. -- (Big buddy biographies)
  ISBN 978-1-60453-971-4
  1. Fanning, Dakota, 1994---Juvenile literature. 2. Actors--United States--Biography--Juvenile literature. I. Title.
  PN2287.F325T54 2010
  791.4302'8092--dc22
  [B]
                          2009032375

Dakota Fanning

Contents

Rising Star

Dakota Fanning is a talented actress. She has been on television and in movies. Dakota is known for acting in *The Cat in the Hat*, *War of the Worlds*, and *Charlotte's Web*.

Dakota became known for her acting skills at a young age. She has received awards for her work.

Family Ties

Hannah Dakota "Dakota" Fanning was born in Conyers, Georgia, on February 23, 1994. Her parents are Joy and Steve Fanning. Dakota has a younger sister named Elle.

Dakota's sister, Elle (*left*), is also an actress.

Did you know...

Dakota's parents could not decide whether to name her Hannah or Dakota. So, they gave her both names.

 Sometimes Dakota is called "Kota."

8

When Dakota was young, her family lived in Conyers. Joy was a tennis player and a homemaker. Steve was a baseball player. Later, he became an electronics salesman.

From a young age, Dakota enjoyed playing pretend. She was good at pretending to be different people. Because of this, her parents thought she could be an actress.

Oregon

California   Nevada

PACIFIC OCEAN

Arizona

Los Angeles

MEXICO

Discovered!

Dakota's family helped her get started in acting. When she was five, Dakota had her first acting job in a **commercial**.

In 2000, Dakota's family moved to Los Angeles, California. There, they hoped Dakota could start an acting **career**. Soon, Dakota got small **roles** in television shows and movies.

Los Angeles is known for its acting opportunities. It was an ideal place for Dakota to seek an acting career.

Like many actors, Dakota often talks to reporters about her work.

Starting Out

In 2001, Dakota had an important **role** in the movie *I Am Sam*. This helped people notice her acting talent. In 2002, Dakota starred in the television **miniseries** *Taken*.

In 2003, *Taken* won an Emmy Award for best miniseries. Emmy Awards are given to the year's best television programs, writers, and actors.

In the Family

Dakota's work as an actress helped her sister, Elle, get acting jobs. Today, they are both known for their acting talent.

Dakota and Elle worked together on *I Am Sam* and *Taken*. Dakota has said she'd like to work with her sister more often.

Dakota is four years older than Elle (*right*).

Like Dakota, Elle (*right*) goes by her middle name. Her full name is Mary Elle Fanning.

Lights! Camera! Action!

Over the years, Dakota has had roles in several successful movies. In 2003, she starred in *Uptown Girls*. Later that year, she played Sally Walden in *The Cat in the Hat*.

By 2005, Dakota was well known for her acting talent. Many people wanted to work with her. That year, Dakota appeared with famous actor Tom Cruise in *War of the Worlds*. This was a very popular movie.

Spencer Breslin was one of Dakota's costars in *The Cat in the Hat*. He played Sally's brother, Conrad.

War of the Worlds is an action movie. Dakota had to run, scream, and act scared for many scenes.

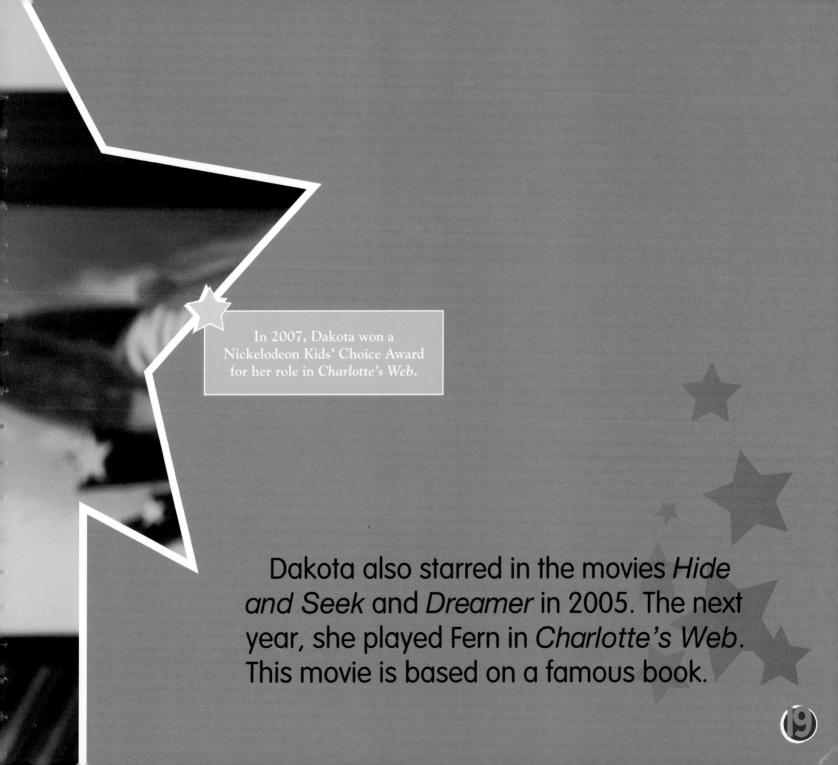

In 2007, Dakota won a Nickelodeon Kids' Choice Award for her role in *Charlotte's Web*.

Dakota also starred in the movies *Hide and Seek* and *Dreamer* in 2005. The next year, she played Fern in *Charlotte's Web*. This movie is based on a famous book.

Charlotte's Web was filmed in Victoria, Australia.

PACIFIC OCEAN

NORTHERN TERRITORY

AUSTRALIA

QUEENSLAND

INDIAN OCEAN

WESTERN AUSTRALIA

SOUTH AUSTRALIA

NEW SOUTH WALES

N W E S

VICTORIA

TASMANIA

SOUTHERN OCEAN

A Working Actress

As an actress, Dakota tours all over the world. She's traveled around North America, Europe, Asia, and Australia. Sometimes she travels to make a movie. Other times, she visits countries to meet fans.

Dakota starred in *Dreamer* with actor Kurt Russell. She enjoyed working with horses while filming the movie.

For her work, Dakota gets to learn special skills. She learned how to ride horses for her **role** in *Dreamer*. For other movies, she studied how to speak Spanish and French.

Dakota invited more than 500 Girl Scouts to a special showing of *Dreamer*. They saw the movie before it came to theaters.

Off the Screen

When Dakota is not working, she spends time with her family and friends. She **knits** and plays the **violin**. And, she is a Girl Scout and a cheerleader.

Dakota also likes to watch movies. Her favorites include *Gone with the Wind* and *Titanic*.

Dakota sometimes knits scarves for her costars. She gave one to Tom Cruise.

Growing Up

As she grew older, Dakota took on more grown-up roles. In 2008, she played Lily Owens in *The Secret Life of Bees*. And in 2009, she had the lead voice role in *Coraline*. Dakota also had a lead part in *Push*.

In *Coraline*, Dakota is the voice of 11-year-old Coraline Jones. The movie is based on a book.

Did you know...

Coraline is a stop-motion film. These films use pictures of 3-D figures and backgrounds. Each picture is slightly different. They are shown very quickly one after another. This makes the figures appear to move.

The cast of *The Secret Life of Bees* included famous singers
Jennifer Hudson (*center*) and Queen Latifah (*right*).

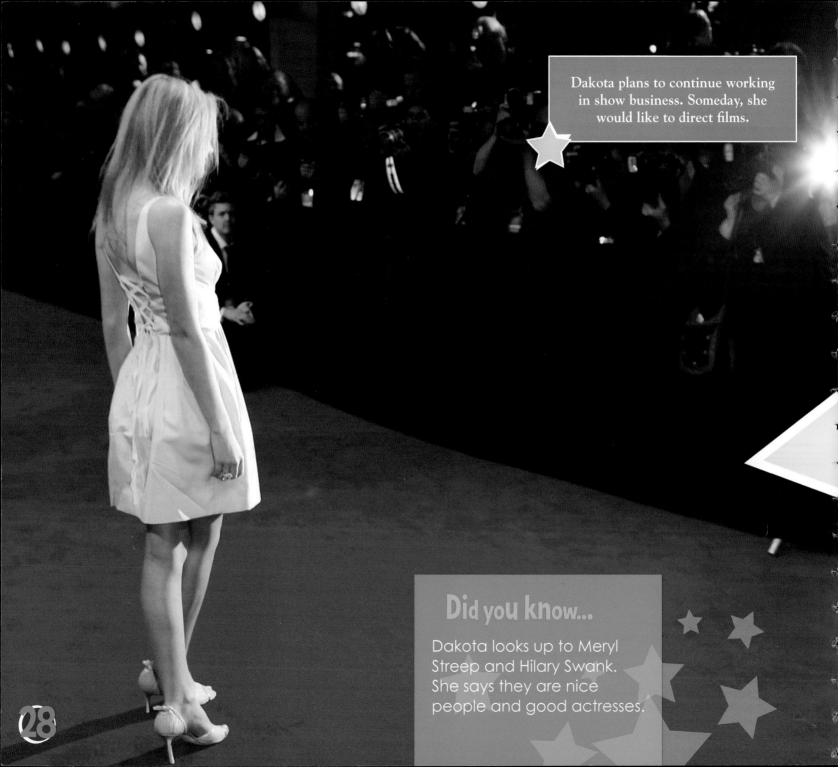

Dakota plans to continue working in show business. Someday, she would like to direct films.

Did you know...

Dakota looks up to Meryl Streep and Hilary Swank. She says they are nice people and good actresses.

Buzz

Dakota's acting **career** continues to grow. In 2009, Dakota acted in *The Twilight Saga: New Moon*. This is part of a popular movie series.

Fans are excited to see what's next for Dakota Fanning. Many believe she has a bright **future**!

Snapshot

⭐**Name**: Hannah Dakota "Dakota" Fanning

⭐**Birthday**: February 23, 1994

⭐**Birthplace**: Conyers, Georgia

⭐**Appearances**: *I Am Sam, Taken, Uptown Girls, The Cat in the Hat, Hide and Seek, War of the Worlds, Dreamer, Charlotte's Web, The Secret Life of Bees, Coraline, Push, The Twilight Saga: New Moon*

Important Words

career work a person does to earn money for a living.

commercial (kuh-MUHR-shuhl) a short message on television or radio that helps sell a product.

future (FYOO-chuhr) a time that has not yet occurred.

knit (NIHT) to make fabric by connecting yarn with a series of loops.

miniseries a long story shown on television in several parts.

role a part an actor plays.

violin a stringed musical instrument played with a bow.

Web Sites

To learn more about Dakota Fanning, visit ABDO Publishing Company online. Web sites about Dakota Fanning are featured on our Book Links page. These links are routinely monitored and updated to provide the most current information available.

www.abdopublishing.com

Index